The Trial and Conv

Infamous Hypocrite John ...

The Surrey Tabernacle Preacher, Borough-road, St. George's Fields,

for an Abominable Offence; Including the Whole of the Evidence;

Tried Before Lord Ellenborough, at the Surrey Assizes, Croydon,

Saturday, August 16, 1817. To Which Is Added, His Life, Confessions,

Notes of One of His Sermons, the Whole of the Love-letters, &c. &c.

Anonymous

Alpha Editions

This edition published in 2024

ISBN : 9789362097583

Design and Setting By
Alpha Editions
www.alphaedis.com
Email - info@alphaedis.com

Contents

SURREY ASSIZES, CROYDON,
Saturday, August 16, 1817.

THE KING v. JOHN CHURCH.

THE Indictment charged, "That the Defendant, late of the parish of St. Mary, Lambeth, in the county of Surrey, on the 26th day of September, in the fifty-seventh year of the reign of George the Third, with force and arms, at the parish aforesaid, in the county aforesaid, in and upon one Adam Foreman, in the peace of God and our said Lord the King, then and there being, did make an assault, and him, the said Adam Foreman, then and there did beat, wound, and ill treat, so that his life was greatly despaired of, with intent, that most horrid and detestable crime, (among Christians not to be named,) with the said Adam Foreman, against the order of nature, then and there feloniously, wickedly, and devilishly, to commit and do, to the great displeasure of Almighty God, to the great damage of the said Adam Foreman, and against the peace," &c.

The second count charged a common assault.

The Defendant pleaded NOT GUILTY.

Counsel for the Prosecution—Mr. MARRYATT and Mr. BOLLAND; Solicitor, Mr. HARMER.

Counsel for the Defendant—Mr. GURNEY and the COMMON SERJEANT.

The Jury being sworn:—Mr. BORLAND opened the indictment, as follows—

May it please your Lordship, Gentlemen of the Jury—The Defendant, John Church, stands indicted for a misdemeanour. He has pleaded Not Guilty, and your charge is to inquire whether he be Guilty or Not Guilty. Hearken to the evidence.

Mr. Marryatt then stated the case on the part of the Prosecution; after which the court proceeded to call witnesses: the first witness called was

ADAM FOREMAN *sworn.*

Examined by Mr. Bolland.—Will be twenty the first day of December next. Is an apprentice to Patrick, the potter, of Vauxhall. Has been with him about five years. Knows the Defendant, John Church, by sight. Has known him about two or three years. Church is a preacher. He, Witness, attended the congregation in the Chapel where Church preaches and has often seen him. Witness sleeps generally at his father's. There are occasions upon which witness sleeps at his master's house when he goes out of town. Church lived by his chapel, in St. George's Fields, the Borough-

Road. Came to take up his abode at Mr. Patrick's the 25th of September, he came to sleep there that night. Witness slept there that night. Does not know whether he (Church) had been there before. Cannot say whether he had seen him there before. Knows that he slept there on the 25th September, and that he, witness, was there. Witness's master that night was out of town; but where he cannot say. Mr. Church, witness's mistress, the children, and the two maid servants, slept in the house that night. There was no other man in the house except himself and Church. Witnesses bed-room was the front parlour on the first floor over the kitchen. It is not a bed-room in common in the house. Witness slept there, because there was no other bed-room that he could sleep in. There was a temporary bed, therefore, put up for him there. Witness retired to rest about one o'clock. The reason for his being up so late was because there was a kiln burning, and he (witness) was obliged to sit up to let the man into the kiln when he came. It was necessary for him to sit up to attend that kiln, and to give the key to the man, Thomas West. Witness went to bed about one o'clock,—went to sleep directly he went to bed. Had not been asleep more than half an hour before he was awoke by some one putting his hands under the bed clothes, and laying hold of his private parts very tight. Witness put his hand out of the bed-clothes, and caught hold of him and asked him who he was? and laid hold of him, as near as he could guess, by the upper part of his arm; felt lower down, and found by the sleeve that he had got a man's shirt on; found the wrist was buttoned; knows very well it was a man; could not tell that from the feel of the flesh. Witness was here asked by *Lord Ellenborough* by what circumstance? and answered because he had got a man's shirt on. The person, in answer to what he said, answered—"Adam, don't you know me? I am your mistress," in a faint voice, like a woman; it was not the voice of his mistress, Mrs. Patrick; witness knew the voice directly he heard it; it was Mr. Church's voice; Church fled the room directly, that is he went out in a hurried step. Witness then got out of bed, and put on his small clothes and shoes, and went to the man up at the kiln. As he opened the door witness saw by the lamp that it was Mr. Church, and he had only his shirt on. The lamp that enabled witness to see the person of Church is outside of the front street door, on the terrace. The lamp throws a light through the fan-light of the hall door. Witness was here asked by *Lord Ellenborough* whether the lamp was at the street door? and he answered, yes. It is a parish lamp; not one of the new lights; nor a gas light. Question by *Lord Ellenborough*—Where were you standing at the time?—I was getting up, my lord. Witness went out of his room. In answer to a question by *Lord Ellenborough*, witness answered, he saw it was Church by the lamp at the street door. Witness was then in bed, sitting up; had not then left his bed; did not open the door; Church did that. Witness saw him go out through that door; and then observed that he had a shirt on. The shirt or dress of a man is much shorter than that of a

- 2 -

woman, and, therefore, he must have seen whether it was a shirt or a shift. It was the shirt of a man witness is sure. Did not see his face at all; his (Church's) back was towards witness. When he was gone, witness got up and put on his small clothes and shoes, and went into the pottery to get the man to come up to the house; told Thomas West of it. Witness was here asked by *Lord Ellenborough* whether West was in the pottery?—and answered, he was; it was the Thomas West that was in the pottery before witness went to bed.

Cross-examined by Mr. Gurney.—The person, whoever it was, opened the door and went out, afterwards shut the door after him. Saw him when he opened the door. There was no light in the room. The light came from a lamp on the Terrace. The lamp is between five and six yards from the door on the Terrace. The Terrace on which witness's master's house is situated, is a row of houses raised above the road. The lamp is upon the Terrace opposite the door. About five or six yards from the door. The light which it gives to the passage is through the fan-light over the door. Did not see the face of the person. Saw that the person had a shirt on. Was rather alarmed, waked out of his sleep in this way. It was not long about. Witness don't know how long he (Church) had been there before witness awoke. Witness went directly to West, who directly came with him and searched the house for thieves. Did not know whether any body had got in or not. Looked at every chamber-door in the house except Mr. Church's and witness's mistress's. Looked at the door of Mr. Church and that of his mistress, but did not open them. They were both of them shut. Did not find any door open. Looked at all the doors in the house, and found them all shut. The maid servant's door was on the jar. All the other doors were shut. After that witness and West searched the house all over. West stopped while the witness put on the remainder of his clothes, witness then went back with West to the pottery, after having locked the door. Told West this story directly, told him that Mr. Church came down into his (witness's) room and behaved in a very indecent manner, that he had laid hold of his private parts, &c. Did not search the house for thieves in particular; but searched if any body was in any of the rooms. *Mr. Bolland* here said, I asked you before whether you did not search the house for thieves; and you answered "Yes," are you right or wrong in that?—I asked you before whether you and he did not search the house for thieves, and you told me that you did?—Witness answered, we searched the house: we looked all over it, to see if there was any body in any of the rooms, but not for thieves in particular. Witness did not think of thieves, because he knew who it was. Did not go into the maid servants' room; only looked in; having found the door open, looked in. The two maids slept in that room; one is witness's sister. The door being ajar, witness pushed it in a little, and saw they were abed. Did not speak to them.

Re-examined by Mr. Bolland.—Witness did not search the house for thieves because he knew who the persons was. The reason of his searching the house was because he wished to be quite right before he made the accusation against Mr. Church. Witness and West found there was no other man in the house but Mr. Church. There was not any door or window open at which any other man could have come in. The light from the Terrace struck through the fan-light or window over the door. It gives a pretty fair light to the hall, it shews a little light up the stairs. It was at the time the person opened the door and went out that witness got this view of his person.

Examined by Lord Ellenborough.—Did not hear Church when he first came into the room. Was awakened by the application of his hand to witness's person. He was standing upon the floor. Witness has not any difficulty in hearing. Witness did not call to him by name, or give him to understand that he knew who he was. Witness saw his (Church's) back as he went out of the room. It appeared to be the height of Mr. Church. Cannot say what height he is. He had a night-cap. Cannot exactly say whether it was a man's night-cap or no. Thinks it was a handkerchief tied round his head. Cannot tell what sort of handkerchief it was. When witness and West searched the house and examined the different doors they went to Mr. Church's door, but did not touch it, nor did they go in. West wanted to go into the room and pull him out. When West wanted to putt him out, witness did not call to him because he was afraid of disturbing his mistress; she would have been very much alarmed. Church never had any conversation with witness, nor did he ever make any overture of this sort to him before this time. There was nothing particular in his manner or conduct towards witness before this time. Witness has not spoken to him at all since. Has attended before a Magistrate with him; spoke in his presence there, but not to him; did not hear him speak before the Magistrate. He did not speak at all before the Magistrate. Witness gave the same account before the Magistrate that he has now done here. Did not know whether it was a handkerchief or a night-cap that was upon his head. There are not any other circumstances from which he, witness, collected that it was a man. The hand did not continue upon witness's person after he awaked at all. The hand was withdrawn then. He said that he was witness's mistress. By the height of the person he saw, witness could ascertain whether it was or was not the height of his mistress, or any of the female part of the house; Mr. Church was a great deal bigger than any body there; witness does not think he is quite six foot; he is a tallish stout man. There was light enough by the lamp that witness has spoken of to see the outline of the man so as to be able to say that he was a tall person. Mrs. Patrick is a very little woman, quite a different person from the person witness saw in the room. The maid, who slept in the room with witness's sister, was about as tall as witness—(*The Witness was about five feet seven*)—not quite so tall. Witness was sure it was not her.—*The Witness withdrew.*

THOMAS WEST, *sworn.*

Examined by Mr. Marryatt. Is workman to Mr. Patrick, the Potter. On the morning of the 26th September last relieved Adam Foreman at the kiln. It was about half past twelve o'clock. Went to the pottery to relieve him. Foreman left witness shortly afterwards, for the purpose of going to bed. It was about an hour before witness saw him again, when witness did see him again he was only part dressed. He had on his small-clothes, his shoes, and one-stocking. He came to witness in a very great fright, and bid him light his candle; he appeared very much alarmed, and bid him light his candle, and come along with him up to the house. He told witness, as they were going along the garden, that Mr. Church has been to him and behaved in a very indecent manner. Did not explain how. He unlocked the door and witness went into the house with him; it was the back door of the house; the outer door; the garden door. When they got to the house he went and put the remainder of his cloths on and they went and searched every room in the house, beginning at the bottom and going to the top, except witness's mistress's room and Mr. Church's; they went into all the rooms except Mr. Church's and Mrs. Patrick's. Did not open the door of either of those two rooms. When they came to Mr. Church's door witness said, "I'll go and pull him out; shall I?" The lad said, "No," for fear of disturbing his mistress. Upon that observation of the lad's, about disturbing his mistress, witness forbore going into the room. Foreman came along with witness into the pottery; came down stairs, locked the back door, and staid with witness the whole of the remainder of the night; he returned with witness to the pottery, and staid till the morning; searched all the rooms of the house, to see if there was any other person in the place; did not find any window or door open, at which any body could have got into the house; they were all close and fastened.

Cross-examined by the Common-Serjeant.—When Foreman came to witness, he told him that Mr. Church had been there; but did not explain what he had done; is quite sure of that.

Lord Ellenborough.—What words did he use?—He only told me that Mr. Church had behaved in a very indecent manner to him.

Witness had never any intimation that there were thieves in the house; did not go to search for thieves in the house. When Foreman told him that Mr. Church had behaved in a very indecent manner to him, witness went to see if there was any other person in the place. Foreman did not tell witness he believed there were thieves in the house. Witness is quite sure Foreman did not explain in what way Church behaved to him. He did not say any thing like—That he came to his bed-side and laid his hand on his private parts. This was on the night of the 25th of September; witness afterwards went before the magistrate, at the same time with Foreman, the apprentice. To Union Hall. Foreman did not, in the course of the morning, when staying with witness, and after he had been to the house, tell witness what Church had done to him, and that he had laid has hand upon his private parts; never told him so, from first to last. Witness cannot say at what time it was that he went before the Magistrate with Foreman; cannot say the day of the month; it was some time afterwards; believes it was six or seven weeks after; the lad then went with his father; the lad generally slept at home at his father's; his father's is about a quarter of a mile from his master's; he slept at his father's the next night but one; it was not till about six or seven weeks after that, they went to the justice; witness did not communicate with Mr. Patrick upon the subject before he went to the justice.

MR. PATRICK *sworn.*

Examined by Mr. Bolland.—Is a potter at Vauxhall. The boy, Foreman, has been with him ever since he has been in the pottery business, between five and six years. He only slept in witness's house occasionally; that is, whenever he (witness) leaves town; and then he has the key of the pottery, there being no other male in the house. Witness was absent from home on the 25th of September last. The boy on that occasion was to steep in his (witness's) house. The bed that had been put up for him was a chair-bed in the front parlour; a temporary bed for a nurse occasionally. Witness knows the Defendant, John Church. He is a Baptist preacher. Witness first became acquainted with him when he came to Vauxhall. Witness attends his chapel, and so became acquainted with him. His residence is adjoining the chapel. In the month of September he came to sleep at witness's house. Witness put a bed up for him. He had complained of ill health occasionally; and thinking that he was ill, witness asked him out of friendship to take a bed at his (witness's) house, supposing that the air would be of service to him. Does not live very close the river. Witness was out from home on the 25th of September. Did not return till the evening of the 26th. The boy, Foreman, made a communication to him the next morning when he saw him. Witness returned on the evening of the 26th.

By Lord Ellenborough.—Then it was the day but one after, namely, the morning of the 27th that the boy made the communication to you?—Yes; my Lord.

Did not see Foreman on the night of witness's return—not to speak with him. On the morning of the 27th he made the communication to witness respecting this transaction. Witness told Foreman he was extremely sorry for what had happened. Witness had had many applications from the congregation, to whom he made it known. It was in consequence of the information they had received from general report, that they applied to witness for authentic information. Several of the congregation made those applications. There was a meeting upon the subject. In consequence of applications made to witness from the congregation, he went to the Defendant, Church. Thinks it was on the 9th of October. There had not before that been a meeting of the congregation, at which witness was present. Did not take any steps between the 27th of September to see Church, and the 9th of October, upon the subject. That was the first communication witness had with Church upon the subject. Church said to him, he took it extremely kind of witness in calling upon him. Witness told him he might take it as he pleased; that he did not come willingly, but that some of his congregation thought that witness ought to see him on the business. Patrick cannot say Church, appeared to be apprized of the subject before witness began; but believes he was apprized from what afterwards occurred. Witness told him he (witness) waited upon him, having seen a letter wherein he denied three particular points of the boy's statement; and witness wished to know what those points were. He said that he denied having hold of the boy, or the boy having told of him; or he, Church, saying that he was the boy's mistress. He admitted he was in the room, but denied laying hold of the boy's private parts; did not state any reason for being in the room at all. He said that he denied three particular points, two of which witness had already named. The other was something that did not occur to witness to be important, and which he did not take any notice of, consequently does not remember it. Witness told him that, of these two points mentioned, the boy was positive, and witness had no reason to doubt any thing that the boy had said, as he had never known him to tell a lie. He said that he was sorry for it, because that confirmed *antient reports*; witness told him it did so; and, of course, that now he should believe all that he had heard heretofore. Witness then wished him a good morning. Did not see him at any time afterwards to speak to him; has seen him, but not spoken to him since. The letter that witness had seen, which he spoke to Church about, was a letter dated the 6th of October, addressed to a Mrs. Hunter. Witness took an exact copy of it. Mr. Harmer has it. Is that the copy? (*A paper put into the witness' hand.*) Yes; it is an exact copy. Witness did not read that copy of the letter to Church; he had. not the copy at that time; only told him he wished to know what the three things were which he could deny, as asserted by the boy; does not recollect the third point; it is not material. He admitted being in the room, but denied the laying hold,—he said, "I was in the room; but I did not lay hold of the boy." Did not say why he was in the room. Witness returned the letter of the 6th of October to Mrs. Hunter. He got it from Mrs. Hunter, and to Mrs. Hunter he returned it.

Cross-examined by Mr. Gurney.—Meant to say that Church said distinctly to witness that he was in the room. Did not mention to any person, after he had see Mr. Church, that he was not implicated in the affair at all. Never said any such thing. Did not give any person an account of the conversation you had with him, and accompany that account with this observation, "He is not at all implicated." Mr. Thomas went to the door of Mr. Church with witness. Thomas is no friend of witness's; witness had only seen him at the door. It was *his* wife and witness's that wished witness to make the application to Mr. Church. Mr. Thomas went with him as far as the door, but did not go in with him. Witness told him briefly what had transpired; it was very short what did transpire. He told Mr. Thomas what had transpired at the interview with Mr. Church, when he came out. Think he told Mr. Thomas that Mr. Church admitted having been in the room, but is not positive as to that point; knows he told him that Mr. Church said he did not lay hold of the boy. Did not answer, on Mr. Thomas asking, "Well, is there any thing against Mr. Church, or not."—"No; he is not at all implicated." Never told him, directly or indirectly, that there was nothing to implicate Mr. Church. Witness did say he would prosecute Mr. Church because he had said disgraceful things of witness's wife, but not for this crime, but for defamation of his wife's character. Don't know that he ever told Mr. Thomas so, but believes he said that, or words to that effect, to other persons. Did not mention that, amongst other things, on that very morning that he had the interview with Mr. Church; some other time he might.

MRS. HUNTER sworn.
Examined by Mr. Marryatt.

Is an attendant amongst the congregation, and a hearer of Mr. Church. Received a letter in the beginning of the month of October, but there was no name to it. There was no place of abode given, nor any thing except the day of the month; could not tell from whom it came; gave it to Mr. Patrick's daughter, who gave it to her father; it was returned to witness again, who took no further notice of it. Witness had a subpœna *duces tecum* so produce it, but was impossible to produce it. After the letter was returned witness took no further notice of it, but put it into a drawer; knows no more than his Lordship what is become of it; looked for it on the Thursday morning before she came, but could find no scraps of it; was not able to find it; was wholly unable to find it; witness searched diligently to find it; is convinced there was no name to it. Has seen Mr. Church's hand-writing, and has seen it written in a different hand, not always alike, but sometimes very different; not to say exactly two different hands, but such a difference in the same hand-writing that she would hardly think it the same; has seen it so different, at times, that she should not at all times, think, it was the same; thinks it was Church's hand-writing, but could not be positive, as there was no name to it; cannot say whether it was or was not; it is not in witness's power. Witness believed, at that time, that it was his hand-writing, and believes it still. When she opened it she was very much struck with the similarity, for it had very much the appearance of his hand-writing; but, as their was not a signature, could not be certain. It had the appearance of his handwriting. Witness's belief now, whether it was or was not his hand-writing, is exactly this same now as it was then. Cannot say. She firmly believes it was his hand-writing, because it was not signed. Did not communicate it to any body but Mr. Patrick. Communicated to Mr. Patrick that she had received a letter from Mr. Church.

Cross-examined by the Common Serjeant. The search which witness made for this letter was not until last Thursday. Witness has no reason to believe that it is in her house, for she did not leave a draw or place unsearched.

Lord Ellenborough.—As far as evidence can go of the loss of an original letter, to let in the copy, we have it in this case; for I asked her whether she made diligent search after the original, and she says, she has made diligent search.

Mr. Patrick examined again by Mr. Marryatt.—Was acquainted in October last with the hand-writing of Mr. Church. The letter from which he made this copy, and which he returned to Mrs. Hunter, was, in his belief, the handwriting of Mr. Church.

Mr. Marryatt.—Now, my Lord, I propose reading this copy of the letter in question.

The following letter was then read in evidence:—

> *October* 6, 1816.
>
> "Dear Mrs. Hunter,
>
> "My heart is already too much affected. Your letter only adds affliction to my bonds. But I forbear. I would have called on you this morning, but I was too low in mind to speak to any friend but Jesus! *There* I am truly comfortable. Pardon me; but I make no remarks on what you have been told. I must bear it, though I am able to contradict *three things* I would rather not. I am only grieved that dear Mrs. P. whom I really loved, that she should try to injure me in the estimation of those who are real friends to my dear children. The thought affects me. Why hurt my poor family? But I am too much depressed to enlarge. I shall never forget their kindness. God will reward them, as he has many who have dealt well to me. But he will resent cruelty in those who have and are still trying to degrade me. Mrs. P. will live to see it. Dear Mrs. Hunter, I am

grieved at heart I cannot relieve your mind. I am truly sorry to lose you as a hearer, because your soul has been blest; and you know both the plague of the heart and the value of Jesus. May he be increasingly present to you in his person, love, and grace! Farewell, my dear kind friend! The Lord Jesus will reward you for your love to me, and your kindness to mine. God is not unrighteous to forget your work of faith and labour of love. With many tears I write this. May we meet in glory, when no enemy shall distress my mind, nor sin nor death shall part us more! I need not remind my dear friend that I am a *Child* of *Peculiar Providence*; and that *heart* of eternal love, and that *arm* of invincible power has protected me—has called me to himself; and for every act of straying, will correct me with *his own hand*, but will resent *every other hand*, sooner or later. This you will live to see.

"*Adieu, dear friend, accept the starting tear,*
And the best wishes of a heart sincere.

"Your's, truly,

"Till we shall meet above."

Mr. Marryatt.—My Lord, that is the case on the part of the prosecution.

MR. GURNEY, on the part of the Defendant, most eloquently addressed the Jury, endeavouring, by observations, to throw some doubt on the testimony of the prosecutor, because he had searched the house after the attack: this, the learned Counsel urged, evinced an uncertainty in the boy's mind, as to the person who had been in his room. That his conduct was unaccountable, in not going into Church's room and questioning him, when he had West to assist him. The learned Counsel also commented on the delay which had taken place before any complaint had been made to a magistrate, and contended, that this circumstance threw discredit on the prosecutor's case, and concluded by observing, that if his client was guilty, his crime was greatly aggravated, because he, as a Minister of the Gospel, was bound to set an example of morality, and intreated the Jury, that as the offence was of so shocking and heinous a nature as to render it improbable that a man in Mr. Church's station could have committed it, that, before they consigned him to eternal infamy, they would be fully satisfied that the testimony against him was unquestionable and conclusive.

The first witness called for the Defendant was

Mr. JOHN THOMAS *sworn.*

Examined by the Common Serjeant.—His name is John Thomas; lives in Prospect-place, West's Square, St. George's Fields; is an appraiser and undertaker; has known Mr. Church a long time; is one of his hearers; is acquainted with Mr. Patrick, but not till the report was made respecting Mr. Church; cannot say he knew him as one of the congregation attending, Mr. Church; was with Mr. Patrick when he went to Mr. Church's house, the 9th of October, a few days after the report; did not go into the house with him, staid outside; had learnt from Mr. Patrick that he was going to Mr. Church's upon the subject of this business; he called upon witness, at his house, to go with him, and told witness he was going to Mr. Church's upon the business of this inquiry; indeed, it was witness's request that he should; Mrs. Thomas went to speak to his wife, and it was at Mrs. Thomas's request and Mrs. Patrick's that he went; he seemed to be a long while in Church's house, not much less than an hour; it was near an hour; when he came out witness put some questions to him, respecting what had passed between him and Mr. Church; witness asked him what Mr. Church had said; he said that Mr. Church did not say anything; that he seemed very much confounded on account of the cause, he supposed, but he said nothing about it, that it would be injurious to the cause of God; he did not say the *cause of God*, witness only supposed he meant the cause of God; did not use the words "cause of God;" he said Mr. Church seemed very much confounded or confused. The rest is all imagination of witness's; both imagined alike; don't know that these were exactly the words; cannot call to his (witness) mind what he (Patrick) did say, but it was conjectured the cause of God, and which they heard afterwards was abused abroad; does not recollect all that passed; Mr. Church had not said anything to Mr. Patrick which Mr. Patrick related to witness; he said Mr. Church seemed very much confused; witness asked Mr. Patrick "what do you mean; why; if you know anything against the man, did you not charge him with it;" he said he did not know; he was not the person; he (Patrick) said, "I don't know: I am not so proper a person as you," or words to the same effect. Witness said to him, "What did he (meaning Church) say respecting the report respecting this transaction?" Witness said to Mr. Patrick, says he, "what did he say respecting the acknowledging the report"—that is, what did Mr. Church say to Mr. Patrick about acknowledging the report that had gone abroad respecting him. He said, "It was false." Patrick said that the report was false. Witness never saw Church upon the subject. When Patrick made witness the answer, he understood that answer to be, that Patrick himself said the report was false. Witness then put other questions to Mr. Patrick. He said, says he, what answer did Mr. Church give respecting its having been reported that he was in liquor—that he made an excuse that he was in liquor? Mr. Patrick said it was false. He said there had been a great deal of exaggeration. Did not after this put any question to Mr. Patrick, whether he, Mr. Patrick, thought that Mr. Church was implicated in the transaction or not. Witness put these words to him—"Why," says he, "you did nothing! Did Mr. Church acknowledge nothing to you?" "No, Sir," says he, "he did not." Then he said Mr. Church had not mentioned a word about it. Did not make any observation to him, or he to witness. Don't recollect any thing in particular witness said, says he, "As you can bring nothing against him, let us pray for him, and if he had the least idea of such a thing; and as you say you cannot bring any thing home to him, and can't prove any thing, that is all we can do. Let us pray that he may not be guilty of such sin."

Lord Ellenborough.—Did you say, pray for him, if he was under any such temptation?—Yes; pray for him, if he was under any such temptation.

Mr. Patrick did not after that deliver any opinion to witness whether he thought Church was implicated in the transaction or not. Did not at any other time see him, and hear him say any thing about this transaction. Nothing more passed at this meeting than what witness has told. Witness afterwards recollected, and asked pardon: he met Patrick in June last, coming over Waterloo-bridge. Did not at first know him; and he spoke to witness, and he said, "My name is Patrick." Witness said, "Mr. Patrick, why what are you doing with Mr. Church?" "Why," says witness, "I hear you have brought something else against him: what is that?"

Lord Ellenborough.—There is no contradiction of Mr. Patrick in this. He was not asked to this (continuation of the answer). "Why," says he, "Sir, I should not have done it, but, that Mr. Church has spoken more disrespectful things respecting Mrs. Patrick." He said he should not have done it, but that Mr. Church had said many disrespectful things of Mrs. Patrick.

Cross-examined by Mr. Marryatt.—Believes it was the Sabbath after the 27th of September that he first heard of this. It was within two or three days after. Heard of the report two or three days after the thing happened. Witness was desirous that Mr. Patrick should call on Mr. Church. He did so, at witness's desire. Believes Mr. Patrick brought the boy to him, and offered to have him brought face to face with Mr. Church. Mr. Patrick called at witness's house in the course of the morning, and he sent him, he said the boy was outside. Mr. Patrick did not particularly wish witness to see the boy; believes he brought the boy to go to Mr. Church's; witness was to go with him, and, therefore, the boy followed. The boy staid outside the door. He walked on the other side of the way, opposite to where witness was. He waited whilst witness waited, they both waited outside ready to go into Mr. Church's when they were wanted. Mr. Patrick was to go in and hear what Mr. Church had to say; and then they were to go in too. He took the boy with him, in order that he might be taken in and see Mr. Church face to face. Witness supposes that was his intention. Witness had no particular acquaintance with Mr. Church, was only one of his hearers, and thought it would be too great a liberty for him to go to him. Mr. Patrick wanted witness to go in alone to Mr. Church first. Don't recollect any thing that he did. Don't know any other reason he had than that for bringing the boy. Don't know that he said that that was his reason. He said he had the boy there. Witness told Patrick he had no particular interest in the business; had no intimacy with Mr. Church, except hearing him: thought he had no business to be interested in the knowledge of the fact, being only a hearer. Thought, therefore, what his visit would be obtrusive; certainly had no interest in it. Saw no necessity for going in and taking the boy, as he, Church, did not acknowledge himself guilty of any thing bad. Did not examine the boy, it being a delicate subject. If Mr. Church had confessed any thing, witness should have it thought it his duty to take the boy and have them face to face. Mr. Church not having confessed any thing, he would not examine the boy; that was his reason for not examining the boy. If he had confessed any thing witness would have taken the boy to have them face to face; his object was to take the boy and have them face to face, if Mr. Church acknowledged the crime. When Mr. Patrick came out and said that Mr. Church did not acknowledge any thing of it he did not think it necessary to have them face to face. Never spoke to the boy. Never asked the boy about this transaction. Mr. Patrick never gave any opinion whether Mr. Church was implicated in the transaction; but in answer to a particular part of the transaction, he said that Mr. Church asserted that it was false. Did not see the letter sent to Mrs. Hunter; about the three points of the boy's statement which Mr. Church said he was able to contradict.

Mr. JAMES REEVES *sworn.*

Examined by the Common Sergeant. Was the Clerk attending the magistrate when the charge was made before him; must refer to the book—Witness produced a book to tell who was the magistrate; it was the minute book in which the entered the proceedings of the day. Mr. Serjeant Sellon appeared to have been the Magistrate on the 19th November, as it appears by the book. Being a charge misdemeanor no account was committed to writing of what the witnesses said; it was merely a note or entry of the names, as follows; "Warrant for a misdeameanor, parties appeared by the Officer, and ordered to find bail."

Cross-examined by Mr. Marryatt.—Mr. Serjeant Sellon was the magistrate by whom the warrant was granted. The oath was administered before the warrant was granted; there had been an *ex-parte* examination to grant the warrant on the oath of the party;—that is in another book left behind; does not know any thing of it. There is a deposition on oath prior to the granting of the warrant.

Re-examined by the Common Serjeant.—Don't take the depositions in cases of misdemeanor in detail. Is not aware of depositions taken in writing in any book which he had not here; was not told to bring it. There was nothing taken down in writing before the warrant was granted. After the warrant was executed, and at the time of the examination, when the Defendant was there, witness took no minutes further than the names of the parties, and what he now produced.

Mr. WOOD *sworn.*

Examined by Mr. Gurney.—Was present at the examination of Mr. Church before the magistrate; is a hatter, near the Elephant and Castle, in St. George's Fields; did not take the testimony of witnesses down in writing. Foreman, the boy, in the account he gave before the magistrate, said he went out to the potter and told the potter that there were thieves in the house, and that the potter and he said the came to search the house. He was asked a question by Mr. Sellon, whether or not he searched the room where Mr. Church slept. He said, no, he did not search that room. Mr. Sellon said, "Why not search the room?" The answer he gave was, that the potter wished to break the door open. Mr. Sellon said, "Did you try the door, to see whether it was open, before the potter talked of breaking it open?" He said, no; he did not wish to disturb his mistress.

Mr. Gurney.—My lord, this is the case of the Defendant.

Mr. Marryatt then replied to the Defendant's case.

Lord Ellenborough proceeded to sum up the evidence on which he commented most ably. With respect to the up the evidence, on which he commented most ably. With respect to the young man searching the house, his Lordship said it shewed a precaution which was highly creditable to the boy, who had also given a good reason for not going into the Defendant's room, namely, that it must have disturbed and alarmed his mistress at that unseasonable hour of the night, and that as to the alleged delay, this seemed to have arisen from the interference of the Defendant's friends; but, although a considerable time elapsed before the prosecutor went to a magistrate, it was clear that he made instant complaint to West, and to his master. His Lordship then adverted to the admission of the Defendant as to being in the boy's room without assigning any reason or motive, and his Lordship asked, what earthly purpose could the Defendant have for visiting this youth in his bed-room in the dead of the night? and, if no honest reason appeared, it was for the jury to say whether the lad's account was not irresistably confirmed by this admission. His Lordship read the letter, before alluded to, throughout, and most emphatically expressed his indignation at sacred names, which ought never to be mentioned but with reverence, being used with disgusting familiarity in such a shocking transaction.

The Jury almost instantly returned a verdict of GUILTY, which gave universal satisfaction to a crowded Court. The trial occupied four hours.

LIFE OF JOHN CHURCH.

The nearer to CHURCH the further from GOD!! *Old English Proverb.*

Dr. Jortin, in his *Adversaria,* very justly remarks, that "a sudden rise from a low station, as it sometimes shews to advantage the virtuous and amiable qualities, which could not exert themselves before, so it more frequently calls forth and exposes to view, those spots of the soul which lay lurking in secret, cramped by penury, and veiled with dissimulation."

JOHN CHURCH, better known as the Obelisk Parson, it appears, was abandoned by his parents, when he was scarcely six weeks old, and left exposed in a basket, with little covering to protect him from the inclemency of the weather, on the steps of St. Andrew's Church, Holborn. In this pitiable state he was found by the overseers of the parish, and sent to the Foundling Hospital; and it was from this circumstance he derived the name of CHURCH. Here he remained until he was nine years old, when a complaint to the Governor's having been made against him by the nurses that he was addicted to improper and disgusting practices, it was thought prudent to apprentice him out at that early age, in order to prevent the morals of the boys being corrupted from so dangerous an example. He must have quitted the hospital at an earlier age than usual, from his evident illiteracy, and the badness of his writing. In general the boys from this institution are distinguished as good scholars. Church was accordingly placed out as an apprentice to a carver and gilder, in the neighbourhood of Blackfriar's Road; but before his time of servitude had expired, he married, and abruptly quitted his master. For a short period he followed his business, and worked for a composition ornament maker, in Tottenham-Court-road; but being of an artful disposition, of lazy habits, and with much hypocritical cant, he at length succeeded in imposing upon several religious persons his great anxiety and desire to become a minister of the Gospel. It appears, he commenced his *pretended* religious career, by taking upon himself the office of a teacher of a sunday school, at that time established in Tottenham Court-road. Thinking that preaching was a more lucrative employment than that in which he was engaged, this hypocritical wretch, together with two other young men, who were also candidates for the gown, hired a garret in Compton-street, Soho, in order to acquire the method of addressing a congregation with confidence. He made a rapid progress in dissimulation, and even at this early period of his religious studies, he laughed in his sleeve at the credulity and ignorance of those persons who were induced to listen to his *pious* harangues. An old chair was the substitute for the pulpit. He now began, as he termed it, "to gammon the old women." Good luck procured him the notice of old Mother Barr, of Orange-street, who being interested in his behalf, allowed him the use of a room of her's, in which he treated her and a few choice labourers in the field of piety, with his rapturous discourses. From this he used to hold forth more publicly. He became acquainted with one GARNET, of notorious memory, who procured him the situation of a preacher at Banbury. It was at this place that he first became obnoxious. But before we proceed further, it may be necessary to inquire by what authority such a man as CHURCH presumed to take upon himself the functions of a minister of the gospel. A man so profligate—so notoriously criminal—come forth to instruct others in religion. It seems, the practice among Dissenters is, that when any man feels a strong desire to become a preacher, he communicates the same to several ministers, who make a strict inquiry into his qualifications as to piety, learning, morals, &c. and if they find these established on satisfactory evidence, they then confer on the candidate a sort of ordination, without which he can have no authority to officiate as a minister of the Gospel. It is evident he must have played the hypocrite in a masterly style, as he did receive an *ordination* at Banbury, in Oxfordshire. But his *real* character soon made its appearance, from his having made several violent attempts upon some young men while at the above place, he was driven out from thence, by the trustees of the chapel in which he preached, and the magistrates, and ordered never to shew his face there again. He hastily decamped, leaving behind him his wife and children, and the police-officers having been sent in pursuit of him, their searches proved fruitless, and it was a long time before he was heard of. He then threw off all controul, and acted *in defiance of all the ordinances of the Dissenting Church!* preaching doctrines tending to encourage licentiousness, and foster the worst of passions. At Colchester he turned the whole congregation against their minister. The mode of healing the consciences of profligate men was practised by the Romish Church before the Reformation, and when it flourished in its rankest state of corruption—when indulgences for sins to be committed, and pardons for sins past, were openly sold for money. The manner in which the Obelisk Preacher conducts the affairs of his chapel bears some resemblance to this practice. He has filled his pockets, it appears, from the money which he has raised by inflaming the passions, and exciting hopes and fears; this *pretender* of piety has even administered the sacrament to persons who were nearly intoxicated with gin! It is said that Church belongs to that sect called ANTINOMIANS, which is thus described by the Rev. John Evans, in his "Sketch of the Denominations of the Christian World:"—"The Antinomian derives his name from ANTI and NOMOS; simplifying, against, and a LAW, his favourite tenet being, that the law is not a rule of life to believers. It is not easy to ascertain what he means by this position, but he seems to carry the doctrine of imputed righteousness of Christ and salvation faith, without works, to such lengths, as to injure, if not wholly destroy, the obligation to moral obedience. Antinomianism may be traced to the period of the Reformation, and its promulgator was John Agricola, originally a disciple of Luther. The Papists, in their disputes with the Protestants of that day, carried the merit of good works to an extravagant length; and this induced some of their opponents to run into the opposite extreme."—"This sect (says the Encyclopædia) sprung up in England during the protectorate of Oliver Cromwell, and extended the system of libertinism much further than Agricola, the disciple of Luther. Some of their teachers expressly maintained, that as the elect cannot fall from grace nor forfeit the divine favour, the wicked actions they commit are not really sinful, nor are they to be considered as instances of their violation of the Divine Law; consequently, they have no occasion to confess their sins, or to break them off by repentance. According to them, it is one of the essential and distinctive characters of the elect that they cannot do any thing displeasing to God, or prohibited by law." It may easily be inferred from such doctrine as the above, the dreadful crime men may be induced to commit, without the horrors of conscience or fear of punishment. From his retreat in the country, it seems, he was called to use his influence in town, by a man of his own disgraceful kind, designated *Kitty Cambric*; and well known at the Swan, in Vere-street. It is notorious from the public exposure of the wretches, who were detected in this street, and brought to punishment, that many of them assumed the name of women, and were absolutely married together, and it appears Church was actually the parson who performed the blasphemous mock ceremony of joining them in the ties of "*holy matrimony*," he being nominated their *chaplain*. He now settled himself at Chapel-court, in the Borough, when his old friend *Garrett* publicly charged him with a wicked and diabolical offence, as the law says, "not to be named amongst Christians," and he was obliged to run away from the accusation. By some fortuitous event he, at length, got possession of the Obelisk Chapel, where he began again to deliver his abominable doctrines; and several young men were obliged to leave him, in consequence of his having used them in a manner too indecent to be mentioned or hinted at. The first document we have is letter dated March 7, 1810, from a person, at Banbury, named Hall, of which the following is a copy:—

> "Honoured Sir—in reply to your letter concerning Mr. C. I can only inform you, there was a report against him of a very scandalous nature; but how far his culpability extends, it is quite out of my power to determine. He was absent from hence when the rumour first spread. The managers of our chapel took great pains to inquire into the origin of such reports, and the result was, they sent Mr. C. positive orders never, on any account, to return to Banbury again; which advice he has hitherto wisely observed. Now, sir, after giving you the above information, I beg leave to

conclude the subject by referring you to your own comment hereon.

(Signed) S. HALL.

Banbury, March 7, 1817."

Then follows a letter from William Clark, of Ipswich, a young man between 19 and 20 years of age, which contains an account of attempts to horrid to be published. The written confession (frightful indeed it is) of this poor simple young man, whose mind was bewildered by the canting exhortations of Church; and the whole of his statements corroborated by the oral testimony of Mr. Wire, who resides at Colchester, and knows Clark very well. The circumstances related by Clark would have furnished ample grounds for a criminal prosecution had he made his complaint *immediately* after the *assault* was committed:—but, suffering under the influence of ignorance and fear, he kept it a secret too long, and afterwards accepted of a pound note from Church. A case was laid before two eminent barristers, to have their opinion whether such a prosecution could be carried on with any prospect of conviction. Their opinion, in writing, is, that after the long concealment of a charge, a jury would pay no attention to his evidence, unless he was confirmed in his story by other evidence.

Extract from the confession of William Clark, of Ipswich.

"Having been called by Providence to Colchester, I went to hear John Church preach in a barn, was invited to Mr. Abbot's; was prevailed upon to sleep with John Church; I did sleep with him three nights; after being enticed to many *imprudencies*, I was under the necessity to resist *certain attempts*, which, if I had complied with, I am fearful must have ruined *both soul and body*: the crime is *too horrid* to relate.

Wm. Clark.

Richard Patmore, J. Ellisdon, C. Wire, H. T. Wire. Witnesses.

P.S. This took place in March last, 1812."

The peace of this poor lad's mind is completely destroyed, so fatally has the event preyed upon him;—so far as to fill the bosom of his aged father with such a spirit of indignation and revenge, that he actually came up to London with a full determination to be the death of him who had thus ruined the peace of his beloved son, while the mother's mind was not less distracted than that of the father's. In consequence of this, the father entered John Church's meeting-house, with two loaded pistols, one in each pocket; but, under the excess of agitation, he fainted away, and was carried out of the place.

The following will cast some light on the preceding:—

"*Colchester, September* 16, 1812.

"SIR,

"Last evening I had an interview with Clark's father, who wishes him to comply with your wishes. I mentioned to him respecting Church's conduct, and I find the last night to be the worst. Likewise that he would have committed the act had not Clark prevented him. The particulars I told you when in London, but find them worse than what I described to you. They are not able to be at any expense; but if the gentlemen wish to prosecute, and to pay Clark's expenses up to London, &c. he will have no objection to come when you please to send. I need only say I wish you to inform the gentlemen, and give me a line.

I am, dear Sir, your's, &c.
C. WIRE."

In addition to the above testimonies, a very long narrative of atrocities committed by JOHN CHURCH; while he resided at Banbury, has been written by a minister at that place; but the facts are too disgusting and shocking to be published.

In the month of April, 1813, a Mr. Webster, who was employed in the house of Messrs. Evans and Co. eminent Hop Merchants, in the Borough, having, this being the time the first public exposure of Church's character took place, asserted his readiness to prove Church's infamy, was immediately seized upon by a fellow of the name of Holmes, and another creature of the name of Shaw, a sort of attorney in St. George's Fields, who had been employed by Church, and dragged to a lock-up-house in the Borough, on a charge of riot, of which the following account appeared in the Morning Chronicle.

Riots at the Obelisk.—Tuesday, a Mr. Webster, who is employed in the house of Messrs. Evans and Co. eminent Hop-Merchants, in the Borough, was charged at Union-Hall, by a person of the name of Shaw, with committing a riot and a breach of the peace, on Sunday morning, at the Obelisk, in St. George's Fields, near the entrance of a chapel belonging to a preacher named John Church. The magistrate said, that as Mr. Birnie, who had, on a former day, heard another case similar to this, was absent, they wished the case might be deferred until next day, and desired Mr. Webster to attend accordingly. The prosecutor observed, that it would be dangerous to allow

Mr. Webster to be at large, and desired that he might be kept in custody or held to bail. The magistrate asked if there was any person present ready to be bail for his appearance. Mr. Robert Bell, the Editor of the *Weekly Despatch*, who accompanied Mr. Webster as his friend, a housekeeper, in Lambeth, said he was ready to bail him. The prosecutor then said, he had also a very serious complaint to make against Mr. Bell, for the article which he published in his last Sunday's newspaper, respecting Mr. Church, and he had one of the papers in his hand. Mr. Bell told the Magistrates that he was ready to meet any complaint of this kind, that he conceived it to be his duty, as one of the guardians of public liberty, and public morals, to send forth the statement in question; that he could prove the truth of every thing he had written and published. The worthy magistrate then asked Mr. Webster if he would promise, on his honour, to attend next day, which Mr. Webster assured him he would do, and retired. It is necessary to mention that Mr. Webster had been kept in a state of imprisonment during the greater part of Sunday, and all Sunday night.

April 7, 1813, Mr. Webster having appeared again before the magistrates, disclosed, in the course of the examination, the fact of Church having, some years since, made an attempt of an abominable nature, on the person of his younger brother, the magistrate, struck with horror, immediately stopt all proceedings against Mr. Webster, and desired his brother to be brought forward. The office was cleared of all persons, except the parties immediately concerned; the brother's deposition was taken, and a warrant was issued for Church to appear there the next day.

On Wednesday, J. Church appeared, in consequence of the warrant issued the day before for his apprehension on a charge of abominable practices, attended by a number of his deluded followers. Mr. W. Webster having deposed as to his attempts on him, Church was ordered to find bail for his appearance at the next Middlesex Sessions, and Mr. Webster bound over to prosecute. The magistrate observed that from the length of time which had elapsed since the offence had been committed, he thought a jury would not feel justified in finding him guilty. Mr. Johnston, a young gentleman of the law, who attended for Mr. Webster, replied, that it was not the time for them to discuss what was likely to be the verdict of a jury;—that he had recommended Mr. Webster to prefer an indictment against Church, and Mr. Webster had come to that resolution; and whatever might be the result of the trial, the evidence relating to the conduct of Church would be of that disgusting nature as to stamp his name with eternal infamy and disgrace. Church's attorney observed that it was a conspiracy amongst another sect to ruin Mr. Church's character. This Mr. Johnson denied and said that it was merely a desire to bring him to merited punishment. Mr. Johnston also said that if Mr. Church acted like a man of prudence, and consulted his own interest, he would desist from preaching until the indictment had been tried, as it would be the means of preventing a breach of the peace, but this he declined; and Shaw; his attorney, said they should follow their own advice. Mr. Johnston informed Church's attorney that it was Mr. Webster's intention to indict, or bring an action against him for an assault and false imprisonment.

On that very evening (incredible as it may appear) this very man held to bail for trial on the most horrid charges, given on oath, had the impudence to go into his chapel and preach to a crowded audience.

On the 6th of June, 1813, the Grand Jury for the county of Middlesex found a bill of indictment against John Church, for his attempt, some years ago, on a lad, named Webster. On the 12th of July following, he was tried and *acquitted.*—If any surprise is manifested at this acquittal, let it be recollected, that this prosecution was ordered by the magistrates, and did not *originate* with the prosecutor, William Webster, on whom the abominable attempt was alleged to have been made (now fourteen years ago). The very mention of the attempt was a mere incidental circumstance arising out of another proceeding then before the Magistrates. Let the reader also take notice of the following sentence:—"The magistrate observed, that from the length of time which had elapsed since the offence had been committed, he thought a Jury would not feel justified in finding him guilty." This William Webster, therefore, must be considered, in all respects, as an unwilling prosecutor. He was supported only by one counsel, then of young standing, (Mr. Adolphus,) who had to struggle against two of the most able advocate (Messrs. Gurney and Alley) in the criminal courts. It appears also that Webster gave his evidence with embarrassment and trepidation, and that he suffered himself to fall into some inconsistencies. With this *solitary* and confused evidence, and after a lapse—after a *silence* of ELEVEN YEARS, was it possible to suppose that a Jury would have found any man guilty? But the verdict did not, in the slightest degree, affect any of the numerous accusations, of a more recent date, which have been made against John Church. From the reports that had gone abroad, that he was addicted to certain abominable propensities, gentlemen in the neighbourhood of the Surrey Theatre, dreading the disgrace of pollution which Christianity might suffer from the immoral character of any of its teachers, investigated these rumours, and the following fact came to light.—James Cook was released from his two year's imprisonment, on the 21st of September, 1813, the landlord of the infamous house in Vere-street. They accidentally met and recognized each other, and a correspondence took place between these *old* acquaintances, on the 13th of October following. A *fac simile* of the letter has been published, in Church's own hand-writing, offering Cook assistance to set up another house, as may be perceived:—

"Dear Sir,

"Lest I should not have time to call or converse with you, as I shall not be alone to Day, I thought it But right to Drop you a Line. I wish you all the success you can desire in getting a house *fit for the business* in the public line; and, as you had a great many acquaintances, they ought not to fail you; if every one acted right, according to there ability, I am sure you would soon accomplish it. As I am By no means Rich, but rather embarrassed, I hope you will accept my mite towards it, 1l. 1s. and you shall have another as convenient, wishing you all prosperity,

"I Remain Your's sincerely,
J. CHURCH."

For Mr. Cook, at Mr. Halladay's, Richmond: buildings, Dean-street.

There is another letter bearing the two-penny post mark of the 20th of October.—It is as follows:—

"Dear Sir,

"I received your note this morning in Bed, as I have contracted such a Dreadful cold Being wet on Tuesday I am very much grieved i have not been able to comply with the request concerning Mr. C— But I shall certainly keep my eye upon him and Do him all the Good it lays in my power where ever he is he knows my Disposition too well to impute any remissness to my conduct But I cannot do impossibilities as I have Lately had and have now Got so many Distressing cases in hand Beside, I will Be sure to call on you as soon as I can—But am not able to day

"I remain Yours, J. CHURCH.

"32 hercules Buildings"

Badly directed to Mr. Oliver, (or Holloway,) No. 6, Richmond's Buildings, Dean-street, Soho.

The following is a narrative which Cook has given of his acquaintance with *Parson Church*; and which was taken down from his own dictation by Mr. E— B—:

"In May, 1810, I was in company with Mr. Yardley and another young man by the name of Ponder. I found after that the said Ponder was a drummer in the Guards; I called

at a house in the London-road, where I saw Mr. Church the
first time in my life: there was at this house about twelve or
fourteen altogether, drinking gin, and Mr. Church handed
me a glass of the same, which I took; Church behaved very
polite to me, and said what a fine fellow I was; he pressed
me very much to stop and get tea with them, for he said he
would call and see me when I was settled in the house in
Vere-street. I stopped a little while, and was about to leave
them, when Church said I should not go before I had tea,
and flung down, a dollar; and a man, by the name of
Gaiscoin, took the money and went for the tea and other
things, but I would not stay: Church came out of the room
with me, and walked with me as far as the turnpike; there
he met another gentleman, which I never saw before, and I
went on and left him for that time; I think it was six or eight
days. I went to live at the Swan, and saw Church again; he
came about three o'clock in the afternoon, and Mr. Yardley
accosted him, "Parson, what are you come to see the
chapel?" He said "Yes, and to preach too." Church asked
me how I was; I said I was not very well: he asked me why
I went away in that shy manner; I told him he was a stranger
to me, and I did not like to be intruding on strange people:
he said I was shy—he did not know what to make of me;
he also pressed me very much to take a walk with him, but
I declined it: he said I must go, but I still declined, and did
not go with him; he staid some time, and joined the
company in the back parlour—persons by the name of Miss
Fox and Miss Kitty Cambrick was among them, and the
Queen of Bohemia. As Mr. Church was going away, he
came to the bar and spoke to me, and said I must take
something to drink, which I did, and he paid for it, and left
the house for that time. In a few days he called again, in the
afternoon, and there was not many people there; he asked
if Yardley was at home; I said he was not; he said he was
very sorry for it; I asked him what he wanted; he said he
came on purpose for me to take a walk with him, but I did
not go: he said he would wait until Yardley came in. Church
said I should do him a great favour if I would take a walk
with him; I would not go—he still pressed me very much to
go: I said I would if he would wait till I had cleaned myself:
he waited more than two hours for me; I went to sleep
because I would not go with him; and in the mean time he
waited so long that he was tired; he sent the waiter to call

me, which he did, and said the Parson wanted me, and had been waiting two hours for me; I said, let him wait, for I should not come; he returned, and said if I would but speak to him, he should go away happy; I found I could not get rid of him—I went down stairs; he said, well, sir, I hope your nap has done you good; I said, I don't know, don't bother me. He said I was very cross to him; I told him there was other men without me; if he wanted to preach, not to preach to me about crossness. He said, well, if that was the case, he was very sorry he had offended me; I told him he had not offended me nor pleased me; but as I was not well, the less any one talked to me the better I liked it; he said, if I was but friends with him, and shake hands with him, he should go away happy. Mr. Yardley said, he never see such a fellow as I was, for I had affronted every body that came to the house. I then shook hands with the Parson, for at that time I did not know his name. He shook hands with me, and we had something to drink, and Mr. Church paid for it and went away. I never saw him till I came out of Newgate; I was talking to Mr. and Mrs. Holloway, and telling them there was a Parson somewhere about St George's Fields, but his name I did not know. He asked me if I should know him if I saw him, I said I should; by that I went to the chapel and saw Mr. Church, and then I asked the people what was the Parson's name; they told me his name was Church. I said he ought to be ashamed of himself to preach there, a ******** and rascal, and left the place, and went home in the greatest pains I ever felt in my life, and was resolved to see him, which I did the next day, and give him one of the hand-bills; and the manner he received me, was like a young man would his sweetheart;—I began my conversation; Well, sir, I suppose you do not know me? He said he did not. I said my name was Cook, that kept the Swan, in Vere-street. He said he thought so, but was not sure: he said why did I not call before and shake hands with a-body. I told him I did not know where he lived, nor I did not know his name until I went to the chapel and found him out. He told me not to make it known that he ever came to my house, for he and Rowland Hill had daggers drawn, and that he should be obliged to indite Hill to clear up his character, and for God's sake do not expose me."—(*Here the narrative breaks off.*)

As an orator, he delivers himself in a full, clear, articulate, tone of voice; but, to criticise his style, or analyse the *substance* of his discourse, would be a fruitless labour; it would be like dissecting a cobweb. Unmeaning rhapsodies and unconnected sentences, through which the faintest gleam of morality is not to be traced, must, from their evanescent nature, set the powers of recollection at defiance, they even escape the lash of contempt. But, to gratify the reader, the following *notes* of a SERMON was taken down in short-hand as he delivered it:—

"God is frequently going forth, and we also are often going to the window to look for him; the more *vile I am* made to appear to the *world*, the more God will *assist* me. Every citizen is a free-born. Many have wondered how I could go through so much trouble. There have been a great many that have wished to see me—I can inform them, I had much rather they had wished to see Christ. People may be laughed at for being fools, but, you may depend upon it, the more God will like them. All that believe not will certainly be damned. The duties of christianity are not to be preached to an ungodly world. John Church is very much spoken of, but they had much better speak of Jesus. The people of the established church feel no spiritual joy. Spiritual discourse is enlivening to the senses. &c. The bread of life is not to be given away to *dogs*. I am not going to turn auctioneer, but I am going to inform you, that, next Lord day, I am going to publish a book, proving that God, the Son, and the Spirit, are all one great God. My sermon will be good news and comfort to all poor sinners. Satan and all his spirits never sleeps; the power of life and death is only in the hands of our Lord Jesus Christ. Devils are allowed to harass the people of God day and night,—no wonder they perplex those they can't destroy. People are mostly liable to fall, in their first love, into awful heresies and temptation. All the Lord's people do not see into the glory of my text—'tis like a jewel in a rock of adamant.— The worst sin was the murdering of God's saints. When I sit in darkness the Lord will be a light unto me. I am never tired of preaching, and, I believe, my dear brethren are never tired of hearing me. Many men laugh at the doctrine of the new birth—are there not many learned doctors that know nothing of it? Let a man come under any circumstances, I will receive him—Don't laugh at the doctrine of inspiration; be wise, it has often been preached by our church. If every one that is saved should be as bright

- 26 -

as the sun, what a place heaven must be, where there will be so many millions! Angels beckon me away, and Christ bids me come. The sight of Christ, you may depend on't, will be worth suffering for. O that I had the voice of an archangel, I would indeed do wonders. I doubt the superiority of one angel over another in heaven—Christ is entirely independent of or with God. We must have the spirit of God before we are his people. Believe in the predestination of eternal life, but not in eternal death; people that suffer were before-hand predestined so to do *by God*. Bad or horrid is the religion of a proud pharisee. The MOB is seldom stirred up but through priests; there is now a case of the very kind: envy bursts forth through jealous and envious neighbouring *priests*, and published by *deists*, there can be nothing to fear; and, I verily believe; that any thing prayed for to Christ will certainly be granted, as has always been the case with me. Let us for ever endeavour to turn every thing, whether good or bad, into good. I do not care who hears me, whether *God* or *man, friends* or *foes, devils* or *angels*, or any thing else; and let them call me an Antinomian again if they please. There must be spiritual life in the soul. I do not believe that God begot Jesus Christ—they say too that Joseph was an impostor, at this very day:— everything that is done against the church is done against Christ; also, that which is done against Christ is done against the church; and anything done against the people of God is done against Christ. It is a most blessed thing that we can throw our burthens upon Christ. That religion that is preached by the people of God is God himself. There can be no going forth until the spirit of God has entered. The Lord Jesus Christ and the people of God are all one. Christ has no sorrow but the people of God must sympathise with him; and the people of God have no affliction but that Christ sympathises with them. This monster—when he was about to preach, would frequently say to his *favorites*;— "Well, I am going tip 'em a gammoning story, my old women would believe the moon to be made of green cheese, If I was to tell them so. And I must tell them something."

In consequence of a respectable young tradesman, in the Borough, Mr. E— B—, who was one of his hearers, becoming disgusted with his hypocrisy, and some attempts he had made upon him, leaving him altogether, he wrote the following beastly epistles:—

Had this wretch received a classical education, one might suppose he had been writing a paraphrase on Virgil's eclogue, beginning with the line—
Formasum Pastor Corydon *Ardebat Alexin.*

Copy of a letter, written by the Rev. John Church, Minister of the Obelisk-Chapel, Blackfriars'-Road, to Mr. E— B—, Rodney-Street, Kent-Street, Borough, dated March 3, 1809.

"Dear Ned,

"May the best blessings be yours in life and in death, while the sweet sensations of real genuine disinterested friendship rules every power of your mind, body, and soul. I can only say I wish you as much captivated with sincere friendship as I am; but we all know our own feelings best. Friendship, those best of names,—affection, those sweetest power,—like some powerful charm that overcomes the mind. I could write much on this subject, but dare not trust you with what I could say, much as I esteem you.—You would consider it unmanly and quite effeminate; and having already proved what human nature is, I must conceal even these emotions of love which I feel. I wish I had the honour of being loved by you as much and in as great a degree as I do you. Sometimes the painful thought of a separation overpowers me; many are now trying at it; but, last night, I told the persons that called on me that, let them insinuate what they would, I would never sacrifice my dear Ned to the shrine of any other friend on earth; and that them you did not like, him should have none of my company at all. I find, dear Ned, many are using all their power to part us; but I hope it will prove in vain on your side: the effect all this has upon me is to make me love you ten times more than ever. I wish opposition may have the same effect upon you in this particular; but I fear not. However, I am confident if you love me now, or any other time, my heart will ever be sat upon you, nor can I forget you till death. Your leaving of me will break my heart,—bring down my poor mind with sorrow to the grave, and wring from my eyes the briny tears, while my busy meddling memory will call to remembrance the few pleasant hours we spent together. I picture to my imagination the affecting scene, the painful thought. I must close the affecting subject; 'tis more than my feelings are able to bear.—My heart is full, my mind is sunk.—I shall be better when I have vented out my grief. Stand fast, my dearest Ned, to me: I shall to you whether you do to me or no; and may we be pardoned, justified, and brought more to the knowledge of Christ. O help me to sing—

When thou, my righteous judge, shall come
To fetch thy ransom'd people home,
    May I among them stand;
Let such a worthless worm as I,
That sometimes am afraid to die,
    Be found at thy right hand.

I love to be among them now,
Before thy gracious feet to bow,
    Though vilest of them all;
But, can I bear the piercing thought,
What if my name should be left out,
    When thou for them should call.

Learn these two verses by heart, and then I will write two more, as they are expressions of mind, fears, sensations, and desires.—I must close, I long to see your dear face again, I long for Sunday morning, till then God bless you.

I remain unalterably thy dear,
thy loving friend.
J. CHURCH."

Another letter was received by Mr. E— B— on the 15th of March, 1809, from Church, without a date, as follows:

"Dear Sir,

"Is this thy kindness to thy once professed much loved friend, surely I never, never, did deserve such cruel treatment at your hands; why not speak to me last night in James-Street when you heard me call, stop! stop! Ned! do, pray do; but cruel, cruel, Ned, deaf to all intreaties—O why was I permitted to pass the door of Mr. Gibbons when you and West were coming out. Why was I permitted to tramp up and down the New Cut after you; I only wanted to speak one bitter, heart-breaking, painful, distressing, word, farewell: I only wanted to pour my sorrows into your bosom, to shake hands with you once more, but I was denied this indulgence. I never, never, thought you would deceive me—O, what an unhappy man am I; the thing that I most feared is come upon me, no excuse can justify such apparent duplicity; O, my distress is great indeed. O my

God! what shall I do? O Christ! O God! support me in this trying hour, what a night am I passing through; I cannot sleep, its near three o'clock; alas! sleep is departed, how great my grief, how bitter my sorrows, the loss of my character is nothing to the loss of one dearer to me than anything else. O let me give vent to tears; but I am too, too, much distressed to cry; O that I could. I feel this like a dagger; never, never, can I forgive the unhappy instrument of my distress in Charlotte-street. Why did my dear friend Edward deceive me? O how my mind was eased on Wednesday night; alas, how distressed on Thursday. I have lost my only bosom friend, nearest, dearest, friend, bosom from bosom torn, how horrid! Ah, dear Suffolk-court, never surely can I see you again. How the Philistines will triumph; there, so would we have it: how Ebeir, Calvin, Thompson, Edwards, Bridgman, all will rejoice, and I have lost my friend, my all in this world, except the other part of myself, my wife, and poor babes; never did I expect this from my dear E— B—. O for a calm mind, that I might sleep till day-light; but no, this I fear will be denied me. How can I bear the piercing thought, parted; a dreadful word, worst of sensations, the only indulgence, the only confident, the only faithful, the only kind and indulgent, sympathising, friend, to lose you. O what a stroke; O what a cut, what shall I do for matter on Sunday; O that I could get some one to preach for me; how can I lift up my head. O sir, if you have a grain of affection left for me, do intreat of God to support me; this is a worse affliction than the loss of my character nine months ago. A man cannot lose his character twice. O, I did think you knew better; I did think I had found one in you that I could not find elsewhere; but no, the first object presented to you, seen suddenly, gained your mind, gained your affections; and I, poor, unhappy, distressed, I, am left to deplore your loss. O for submission, but I am distressed; woe is me. O that I had never, never, known you, then I should never feel what I do; but I thank you for your company hitherto, I have enjoyed it four months exactly, but this is over for ever; miserable as I am, I wish you well for ever, for ever. I write in the bitterness of my soul which I feel. May you never be cursed with the feelings I possess as long as you live. What a day I have before me! I cannot go out of my house till Sunday morning. How can I conceal my grief from my dear wife?—how shall I hide it?—what shall I say?—I am miserable, nor can I surmount the shock at all. I have no friend to pour out my sorrows to now, I wish I had; I am sorry you are so easily duped by any to answer their purposes: my paper is full, my paper is full, my heart is worse; God help me! Lord God support me! What shall I do, dear God! O Lord have mercy on me! I must close; this comes from your ever loving, but distressed,

J. CHURCH."

In addition to the confession made to Mrs. Hunter, the following confessional letter from Church, was sent to the great surprise of the Rev. Mr. L—, two days after the offence had been committed. It appears that Church was but very slightly known to the above gentleman, in consequence of some money transactions having passed between them:—

DEAR SIR—Surely upon the reception of this short note you will say, ah, *Church* is like all the rest of the parsons, promise much and do little, yea nothing: to your note I can only with a pained heart reply *I cannot indeed*—I can scarcely write this note, my soul is too deeply pierced. About eight or nine years ago Dr. Draper left the church in the Borough and God opened Chapel-court for me, many attended and have been blest, now a singular providence, but a most distressing one, has occurred to take me shortly from my dear, dear family and beloved congregation. But God has sent Mr. L— to preach all the truth to my poor dispersed flock, at least so it appears to me, and I would do all the good to promote the success of Mr. L— that my poor people might not be starved till I return to them in peace, which may be many months. My heart is broken, my enemies have ruined me at last, and I shall never, never surmount it, an unpleasant affair happening at Vauxall, is added too, and I must take the consequences: no arm can help, relieve, or deliver, but the Lord's, and I feel persuaded the Lord will *not* judge my feelings if you can. I shall secretly come and hear you, to get all the good I can to a heart deprest, disconsolate, and full of woe. Oh, the joy of my enemies! Oh the distress of my friends! Oh, my poor heart! Let a sigh go up to God for me when you can.

Your's, in the utmost distress,

J. C.

The following bad character has been given of Church by Mr. and Mrs. Gee, of the New Cut, who keep a cake-shop, where he once lodged:—

"Mr Church, the minister, lodged at our house a year and a half, and left last year at Lady Day.

"We were in hopes that we were about to have a godly praying minster in our house; and to be sure the first night he had somewhat like a prayer, and that once afterwards were the only times he ever went to family prayer in our house. Nor could they have any prayer, as he would be frequently out almost all hours of the night, and would lie in bed till ten in the morning. Several times he and his wife would have skirmishings and fightings between themselves, while the children would be left to run about the streets out of school hours, and allowed to keep company with children that would swear in our hearing most shockingly. His children were always left to be very dirty, and would be sent sometimes three or four times in a morning for spirituous liquors of all sorts. As for reading good books, or even the Bible, he scarce ever thought of it, but would spend a deal of his time in loose and vain talk, in walking about, and fawning upon young men, that was his chief delight.

"Sundays and working days were all alike to them, for they would send out to buy liquors, and whatever else they wanted, on Sundays as well as other days.

"The house would be frequently more like a playhouse (I might say a bawdy house) than a minister's house, were a set of young people would come and behave more indecently than ought to be mentioned. Even one Sunday morning they made such an uproar as that they broke one of the windows, after that they would go with him to his chapel, and, after that, he would give the sacrament to such disorderly people, let their characters be ever so loose.

"He was always ready to go fast enough out to dinner or supper where he could get good eating and drinking, but poor people might send to him from their sick bed times and times before he would come to them. Seeing so much of his inconsistencies and shocking filthiness in their rooms, (though they always paid their rent,) we were determined to give them warning to quit our house, and we do not think that a worse man or woman ever came into any house before, especially as Mr. Church pretended to preach the gospel; such hypocrites are much worse than others, and, besides this, we never heard a man tell lies so fast in all our lives. It is a great grief to us that ever we went to hear him preach, or suffered him to stop so long in our house."

GEORGE AND FRANCES GEE.

It appears from the testimony of George Tarrier, and James Russell, of Redcross-street; of Richard Jessop, of Castle-street; and William Williams of the Mint; that the *Rev. John Church*, on the 16th of November, 1809, also attended at the funeral of Richard Oakden, a clerk in the Bank, who was hung before Newgate, for an abominable offence, on 14th November, 1809. This *pious* minister and his partizans returned to the Hat and Feathers, Gravel-lane, kept by a Mr. Richardson, where the funeral set out from, to partake of a jovial dinner. His conduct here, it seems, was beyond description.

It is averred, that his wife, upon hearing the infamy of his conduct took to drinking, to avoid reflection, which soon occasioned her death. But, within the last three months since, he has been charged with the above detestable offence, in order (we presume under the mask of hypocrisy,) to rescue, in some degree, his character from the public odium with which it had been marked, he has been induced to marry a respectable woman, who kept a seminary for young ladies at Hammersmith. The verdict of "Guilty" had been scarcely pronounced, when the relatives of the children, with the greatest promptitude possible, took them all away from the said school.

Some time previous to the commission of the offence for which Church has been at last convicted he made an attempt, in the open street, on the person of a poor Frenchman, who had him conveyed to the watchhouse, where a long examination took place, but the proof not being very conclusive, the affair was hushed up.

Since his conviction, Church has resided at the house of *a friend*, where *his followers* are admitted to see him on producing a card signed by himself, on which are inscribed certain texts of scripture. Will this wretch never cease blaspheming the holy scriptures by his appropriation of them!

It may not be improper to state one of the tricks made use of to threw the prosecutor off his guard. A limb of the law, it appears, of the *Jewish* persuasion, *gratuitously* offered to conduct the prosecution for the young man; but upon a refusal being given him, on account of Mr. HARMER being selected for that purpose, it was ultimately discovered that this *philanthropic* Israelite had been exerting himself towards exculpating Church, with all the ingenuity he was master of in his defence, from the heinous offence alleged against him. The "laws delay" was resorted to, but only to put off the trial till the next assizes, but the expenses materially increased, as a means of deterring the prosecutor from proceeding. It is, however, lamentable to observe, that the charges in bringing such a wretch to justice, should amount to eighty or ninety pounds!

From the acknowledgement of this monster himself, the profits of this *precious* recepticle produced him from £1000 to £1200 annually.

At length, this precious hypocrite, who has so long set all decency at defiance, by public preaching, notwithstanding his diabolical well known propensities, has been found guilty of the crime he has so long (and so numerously) been charged with. Much as it might be wished that such a monster, under the disguise of that sacred habit, which at all times is entitled to reverence, should be consigned with his crimes to oblivion. But such suppression would be doing a serious injury to public morals. Delicacy at all times ought to be a paramount consideration, but there are cases in which a great deal more injury both to morals and liberty may arise from the suppression than the exposure of indecencies. This we apprehend to be one of that sort, and great care has been taken to avoid entering into any disgusting particulars. It is due to the community at large that such a dangerous character should be exposed to society, and it is equally important to that sacred body, who can only rise or fall in public estimation from their good conduct.

He will be brought up the first day of next term to receive judgement in the Court of King's Bench. Mr. Gurney we understand, although he so ably and eloquently defended the guilty monster, Church, undertook his cause with the greatest reluctance.

APPENDIX.

Since the publication of our third edition, we have received the following curious epistle, in *print*, from the Rev. J. L. Garrett, whose name is mentioned by us, p. 29 and p. 31. This letter, we understand, has been very industriously circulated amongst his friends and acquaintance. Although we cannot comply with the reverend gentleman's request, to erase his name from our pages, as it does not appear that we have stated any thing materially incorrect, we will do him the justice to print his vindication of himself, a mode of proceeding which we think will serve the reverend gentleman's interests more than any other, our work having so unprecedented a sale, that it must carry it into every channel necessary for the Reverend Professor of Natural Philosophy's vindication, of whose *reformation* we are truly happy to hear.

THE REV. J. L. GARRETT'S VINDICATION.

Letter addressed by the Rev. J. L. GARRETT, *Professor of Natural Philosophy, &c. to the Publisher of a Six-penny Pamphlet, intituled,* "*The Life and Trial of* Mr. JOHN CHURCH."

DEAR SIR,

As bigotry, superstition, and misguided zeal, those dreadful sources of violence, wasting, and destruction, which once too often actuated both my tongue and pen, have now, through divine Grace, for several years, ceased to form any trait in my deportment; you will, I trust, allow me the humble claim, of having that erased from your pamphlet, which a better use of my reason has so evidently erased from my conduct.

Rest assured, I most sincerely wish success to every laudable effort you can exert to suppress vice, but particularly vices so extremity disgraceful to human nature—but have the goodness, Sir, to understand that I never, in my life, was what your pamphlet calls me, a friend or acquaintance of the person you allude to, nor *never* had any thing *to do with him*, but what was *forced on me* by *his own insinuations*, which principally were carried on with some of my people in Lant-street while I was out of town.

I also remark that I had no hand in getting him into Banbury; and can only say, would to God that those things which drove him out had been followed by sincere repentance, then I think I should have been one of the first to have administered the consolation of the gospel; but as things are, I shall leave the detection and suppression of vice in abler hands than my own, with this prayer, that "That truly wretched man, may yet be brought with sincere repentance to the feet of Jesus, obtain mercy, and, under the influence and operation of the holy spirit, gain the completest mastery over a nature so awfully depraved, and thus prove that nothing is too hard for God."

While I remain,

Your's respectfully,
J. L. GARRETT.

Philosophical Museum,
    Mile End, Aug. 28th, 1817.

P.S. Since I sent my note to the press, my friends have manifested some objections to the gentleness of my remonstrances, under circumstances so truly aggravating, as that of having my name at all mentioned in the details of such a filthy concern; and as I have occasionally the instruction of noblemen's sons, of the first respectability, I must, under every consideration, insist on its being immediately withdrawn.—But, if humanity should dispose you to dispense with my name, in this instance, without further trouble, it shall certainly be at your service, whenever you feel disposed seriously to argue the possibility of one bigot in a hundred being brought to the right use of his reason.

You will, I trust, excuse the shortness of this address, as my own paralytic debility, accompanied with a death in my family, which has not yet advanced to interment, forbids me to say more.

To Mr. J. Fairburn,
    Publisher, &c.

CHURCH BURNT IN EFFIGY!

We are informed by a most respectable follower of and believer in, John Church, one who gave evidence on his trial in his favour, and whose name we will, if required, give up to satisfy the most credulous of its authenticity, that on Monday evening last, after a visit to his residence, adjoining the Tabernacle, in the Borough-road, he returned to Rock-House, Hammersmith, which he had no sooner entered than the mob, having gained a knowledge of his being there, attacked with mud, filth, and other missile annoyances, and presently broke all the windows, expressing their indignation at Church's most abominable atrocities; meanwhile, by groans, hisses, and all sorts of execrations, they having previously drest up an effigy of him, in a black silk gown, with a painted *Church* placed on each side, that the most dull might be informed whom it was meant to represent, paraded with it all through the village, when they finally burnt it to typify those *Gomorrah fires*, which, in the absence of a timely and sincere repentance, we are taught to believe will be the lot of the original in that place where fire is never quenched. Of this repentance we are sorry to observe no signs at present, but we trust the forth-coming punishment (most probably *solitary confinement*) will give him leisure to reflect on his atrocities and awaken him to a due sense of their enormities: truly happy shall we be to hear that the retribution of an earthly judge has shewn him the greater danger in which he stands with regard to his heavenly one.

AN EPISTLE

From the DEVIL *to his Friend mid Follower* JOHN CHURCH.

OH, say not, JOHN CHURCH,
I've left you *in the lurch*,
　　When *your life in my service you've past*;
Though *I seem to forsake*,
My dear John, do not *quake*,
　　I'll be sure to *stick to you at last*.

You know that *Old Nick*
Still is sure those to *trick*,
　　Who think they *as deep are as he*;
And *he*, still, John, it proves,
Chaseneth those he best loves,
　　And *he loves none so dearly as thee*.

Besides, John, I thought
If I let you be caught
　　In your tricks here on earth, 'twould be well;
For 'twould serve for a taste
Of the joys you must haste
　　To enjoy with me, Johnny, in h—.

And then, John, your *preaching*,
And *spiritual teaching*,
　　Had almost grown *too great a joke*;
To those who knew you,
And they were not a few,
　　Who still laugh'd as on gospel you spoke.

True, you still rail'd at me,
John, *sans ceremonie*,
　　And no one thought me your sworn brother;
Like rouges in-grain true,
Who their tricks to pursue,
　　Still behind their backs backbite each other.

Like me you wear black,
My dear John, on your back,
　　Then, hasten, dear John, to come down;
Guilt's ne'er look'd on so well,

My dear Johnny, in h—,
  As when *clad in a minister's gown.*

We are hypocrites both,
To deceive nothing loth,
  In short we're just form'd for each other;
Then *come Johnny, do,*
Or I must come for you,—
  Oh, come to Old Nick, your dear brother.

You shall be treated well,
Dearest Johnny, in h—,
  You on *sulphur and brimstone* shall feast;
We'll with *fires keep you warm,*
And do all things to charm;
  As befits so illustrious a guest.

In h—, John, you'll meet
Many friends from *Vere-Street,*
  Which quite cosey and handy will be;
For their *chaplain* in h—
You may be, John, as well
  As on earth you us'd one time, be.

True, John, scripture you quote,
Like a parrot, by rote,
  So too many other men do;
And then 'tis well known
Almost to every one,
  I, the devil, can quote scripture too.

Thy locks all so lank,
And thy chops all so blank,
  And thy hoarse nasal twangings to boot;
Finely humm'd all the folks;
But adieu to such jokes,
  For, like me, you've now shewn *cloven foot.*

THE END.

Milton Keynes UK
Ingram Content Group UK Ltd.
UKHW030945071024
449371UK00016B/581